Introduction

Creativity sometimes has to be squeezed into our busy schedules, and there are only so many free hours available for doing the things that we love. We have put together this book of 14 projects to help you get the most out of your quilting time. These quilts can all be pieced in a day or two, making this a perfect book to have on hand for a rainy afternoon! We hope that you take advantage of these wonderful patterns and find a way to fit them into your busy schedule. You will be glad you did!

Enjoy!

Table of Contents

DESIGNED & QUILTED BY TRICIA LYNN MALONEY

Jelly Jar Runner

Four 16-Patch blocks set on point make this gorgeous table runner something special.

SPECIFICATIONS
Skill Level: Beginner
Runner Size: 49⅜" x 15⅜"
Block Size: 8" x 8" finished
Number of Blocks: 4

MATERIALS

- 16 coordinating precut 5" squares*
- ⅜ yard gray check*
- ⅜ yard aqua floral*
- ½ yard yellow dot*
- Backing to size
- Batting to size
- Thread
- Basic sewing tools and supplies

Sweet Prairie fabric collection from Riley Blake Designs used to make sample.

CUTTING

From 5" squares:

Cut each 5" square into 4 (2½")
A squares (64 total).

From gray check:

- Cut 4 (2¼" by fabric width) binding strips.

From aqua floral:

- Cut 4 (2½" by fabric width) strips.
  Subcut 1 strip into 2 (2½" x 15⅞")
  E strips. Set aside remaining
  3 strips for D.

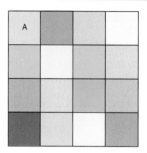

16-Patch
8" x 8" Finished Block
Make 4

From yellow dot:
- Cut 1 (12⅝" by fabric width) strip. Subcut strip into 2 (12⅝") B squares and 2 (6½") C squares. Cut each B square on both diagonals to make 8 B triangles and each C square in half on 1 diagonal to make 4 C triangles. Set aside 2 B triangles for another project.

Here's a Tip

Scraps cut into 2½" strips or squares may be used instead of the 5" squares. Cut extra squares so you can move them around when piecing, if necessary.

COMPLETING THE BLOCKS

1. To complete one 16-Patch block, join four A squares to make a row; press. Repeat to make a total of four rows.

2. Join the rows referring to the block drawing to complete one 16-Patch block; press.

3. Repeat steps 1 and 2 to complete a total of four 16-Patch blocks.

COMPLETING THE RUNNER

Refer to the Assembly Diagram for construction steps.

1. Arrange and join one 16-Patch block with two B triangles to make a diagonal row; press. Repeat to make a second diagonal row.

2. Sew a B triangle to one side and C triangles to two adjacent sides of one 16-Patch block to make an end unit; press. Repeat to make a second end unit.

3. Arrange and join the two diagonal rows with the end units to complete the pieced center; press.

4. Join the D strips on the short ends to make one long strip. Subcut strip into two 2½" x 45⅞" D strips.

5. Sew the D strips to opposite long sides and E strips to opposite short ends of the pieced center to complete the runner top; press.

6. Create a quilt sandwich referring to Quilting Basics on page 48.

7. Quilt as desired.

8. Bind edges referring to Quilting Basics on page 48 to finish. ●

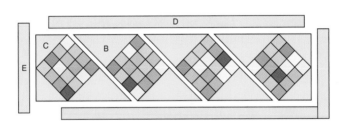

Jelly Jar Runner
Assembly Diagram 49⅜" x 15⅜"

Logjam Table Topper

SPECIFICATIONS
Skill Level: Beginner
Table Topper Size: 23½" x 23½"
Block Size: 9" x 9" finished
Number of Blocks: 4

By simply arranging four Log Cabin blocks to set off the darks and the lights, you can create an interesting table topper for any table and any style.

MATERIALS

- ⅛ yard each of 2 each gray, brown and black batiks*
- ¼ yard light brown batik*
- ½ yard black solid*
- ⅝ yard cream solid*
- Backing to size
- Batting to size*
- Thread
- Basic sewing tools and supplies

Fabrics from Hoffman California Fabrics; 80/20 batting from Hobbs used to make sample.

CUTTING

From gray, brown & black batiks:
- Cut 1 (1½" by fabric width) strip each fabric. **Note:** *All pieces of 1 letter are cut from the same fabric in the sample topper.*

    Subcut 1 gray strip into 4 (1½" x 4½") D strips and the remaining gray strip into 4 (1½" x 5½") E strips.

    Subcut 1 brown strip into 4 (1½" x 6½") H strips and the remaining brown strip into 4 (1½" x 7½") I strips.

    Subcut 1 black strip into 4 (1½" x 8½") L strips and the remaining black strip into 4 (1½" x 9½") M strips.

From light brown batik:
- Cut 4 (1¼" by fabric width) strips. Trim strips to make 4 (1¼" x 24") P strips.

From black solid:
- Cut 1 (3½" by fabric width) strip. Subcut strip into 4 (3½") A squares.
- Cut 3 (2½" by fabric width) binding strips.

From cream solid:
- Cut 4 (1½" by fabric width) strips. Subcut strips into 4 each 1½" x 3½" B, 1½" x 4½" C, 1½" x 5½" F, 1½" x 6½" G, 1½" x 7½" J, and 1½" x 8½" K strips.
- Cut 3 (3¼" by fabric width) strips. Subcut strips into 2 each 3¼" x 18½" N and 3¼" x 24" O strips.

COMPLETING THE BLOCKS

1. To complete one Log Cabin block, select one each piece A–M.

2. Referring to Figure 1, sew B to A; press. Add C; press.

3. Sew D and E to the remaining sides of A to complete one round as shown in Figure 2; press.

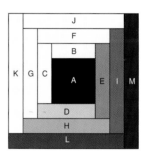

Log Cabin
9" x 9" Finished Block
Make 4

4. Continue adding pieces in alphabetical order until the block has three pieces on each side of the center A square to complete one Log Cabin block as shown in Figure 3; press after adding each strip.

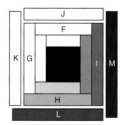

Figure 3

5. Repeat steps 1–4 to complete a total of four Log Cabin blocks.

Figure 1   **Figure 2**

COMPLETING THE TABLE TOPPER

Refer to the Assembly Diagram for completing the pieced top.

1. Arrange and join two Log Cabin blocks to make a row; press. Repeat to make a second row.

2. Join the rows to complete the pieced center; press.

3. Sew N strips to opposite sides and O strips to the top and bottom of the pieced center; press.

4. Create a quilt sandwich referring to Quilting Basics on page 48.

5. Quilt as desired.

6. Fold each P strip in half with wrong sides together along length to make four P flange strips.

7. Pin a P flange strip to opposite sides, and top and bottom of the quilted topper with raw edges even and folded edge toward the center as shown in Figure 4. Machine-baste ⅛" from edge to hold in place.

Figure 4

8. Bind edges referring to Quilting Basics on page 48 to finish. ●

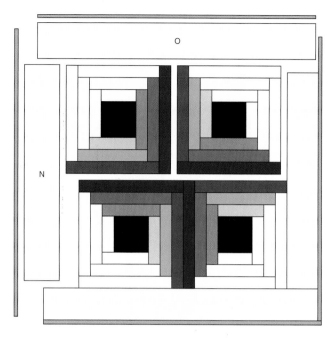

Logjam Table Topper
Assembly Diagram 23½" x 23½"

Splitting Hairs Table Runner

This simple yet elegant table runner may also be made with leftover precut 2½" strips from previous projects. It's a great way to use scraps and show off the fabrics you love.

SPECIFICATIONS
Skill Level: Beginner
Runner Size: 53" x 23"
Block Size: 5" x 5" finished
Number of Blocks: 24

MATERIALS

- 10–12 coordinating 2½" by fabric width strips*
- 1⅝ yards white solid
- Backing to size
- Batting to size*
- Thread
- Basic sewing tools and supplies

Java Batiks from Maywood Studio; Hobbs batting used to make sample.

CUTTING

From 2½" by fabric width strips:

- Cut 48 (2½" x 5½") A rectangles.
- Cut 36 (1½") C squares.

From white solid:

- Cut 4 (5½" by fabric width) strips. Subcut strips into 83 (1½" x 5½") B rectangles.
- Cut 4 (2½" by fabric width) strips. Subcut 1 strip into 2 (2½" x 19") D strips. Set aside 3 remaining strips for E.
- Cut 5 (2¼" by fabric width) binding strips.

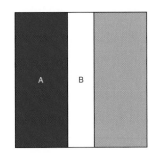

Split
5" x 5" Finished Block
Make 24

COMPLETING THE BLOCKS

1. Sew a B rectangle between two A rectangles to complete one Split block referring to the block drawing; press.

2. Repeat step 1 to complete a total of 24 Split blocks.

COMPLETING THE RUNNER

Refer to the Assembly Diagram for construction steps.

1. Join three Split blocks with four B rectangles to make a vertical X row; press. Repeat to make a total of four X rows.

2. Repeat step 1 to make four Y rows, turning each block the opposite way from blocks in the X rows.

3. Join three B rectangles and four C squares to make a sashing row; press. Repeat to make a total of nine sashing rows.

4. Join the X and Y rows with the sashing rows to complete the pieced center; press.

5. Join the E strips on the short ends to make one long strip; press. Subcut strip into two 2½" x 53½" E strips.

6. Sew D strips to the short ends and E strips to opposite long sides of the pieced center to complete the runner top; press.

7. Create a quilt sandwich referring to Quilting Basics on page 48.

8. Quilt as desired.

9. Bind edges referring to Quilting Basics on page 48 to finish. ●

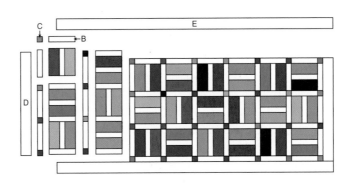

Splitting Hairs Table Runner
Assembly Diagram 53" x 23"

Monochromatic Table Runner

Whatever color you choose, this table runner will stand out on your table and showcase your quilting talent.

SPECIFICATIONS

Skill Level: Beginner
Runner Size: 40½" x 22½"
Block Size: 4½" x 4½" finished
Number of Blocks: 18

MATERIALS

- 18 (2" x 16") strips assorted dark blue prints
- ⅜ yard navy solid
- 1 yard white solid
- Backing to size
- Batting to size*
- Thread
- Basic sewing tools and supplies

Warm & White batting from The Warm Company used to make sample.

CUTTING

From each dark blue print strip:

- Cut 2 each 2" A squares and 2" x 5" B rectangles.

From navy solid:

- Cut 4 (2¼" by fabric width) binding strips.

From white solid:

- Cut 5 (2" by fabric width) strips.
  Subcut strips into 18 (2") C squares, 15 (2" x 5") D rectangles and 2 (2" x 35") E strips.
- Cut 4 (3½" by fabric width) strips.
  Subcut 1 strip into 2 (3½" x 17") F strips.
  Set aside remaining 3 strips for G.

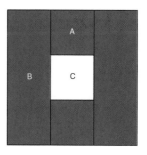

Square
4¹/₂" x 4¹/₂" Finished Block
Make 18

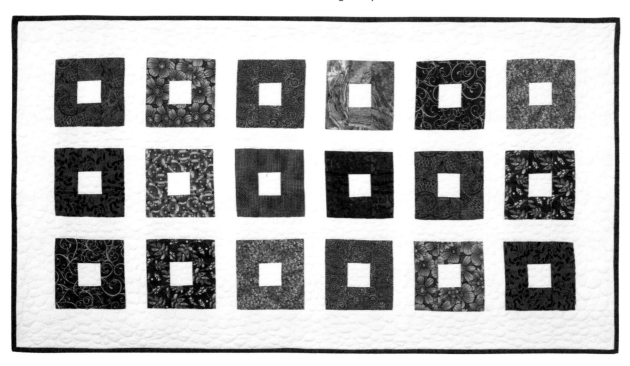

COMPLETING THE BLOCKS

1. To complete one Square block, select two each matching A and B pieces and one C square.

2. Sew A to opposite sides of C to make an A-C unit as shown in Figure 1; press.

A-C Unit

Figure 1

3. Sew B to opposite long sides of the A-C unit to complete one Square block as shown in Figure 2; press.

Figure 2

4. Repeat steps 1–3 to complete a total of 18 Square blocks.

COMPLETING THE RUNNER

Refer to the Assembly Diagram for construction steps.

1. Join six Square blocks with five D rectangles to make a row; press. Repeat to make a total of three rows.

2. Join the rows with the two E strips to complete the runner center; press.

3. Sew F strips to opposite short ends of the runner center; press.

4. Join the G strips on the short ends to make one long strip. Subcut strip into two 3½" x 41" G strips.

5. Sew G strips to opposite long sides of the runner center to complete the runner top; press.

6. Create a quilt sandwich referring to Quilting Basics on page 48.

7. Quilt as desired.

8. Bind edges referring to Quilting Basics on page 48 to finish. ●

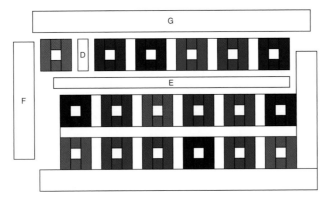

Monochromatic Table Runner
Assembly Diagram 40½" x 22½"

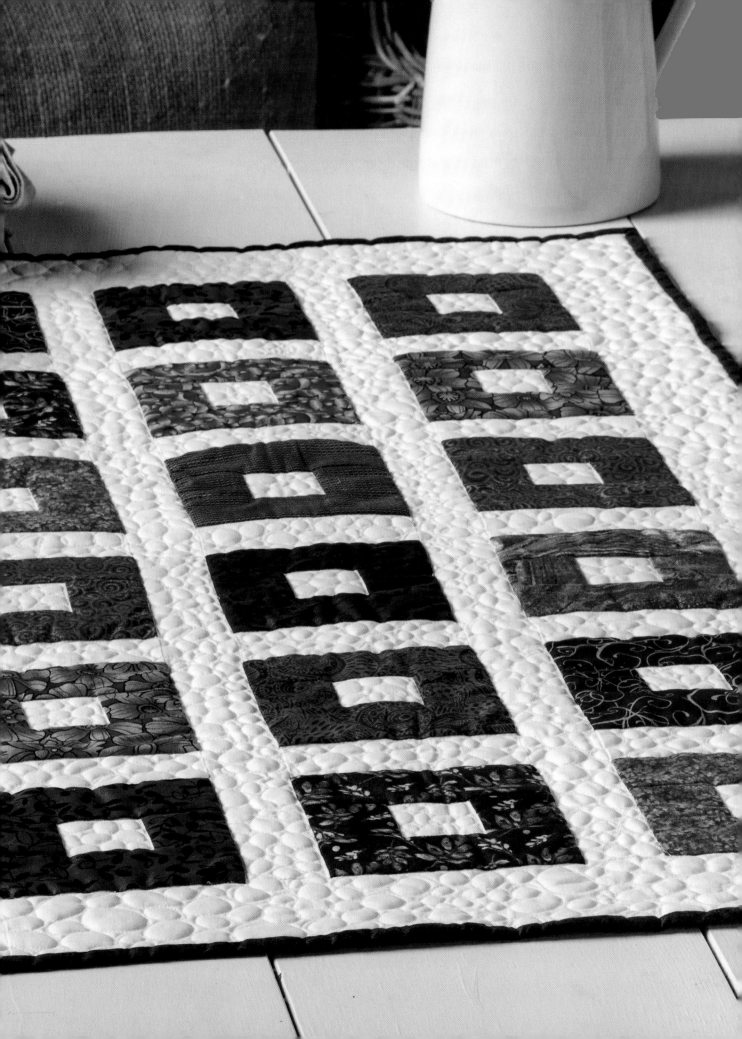

DESIGN BY DENISE RUSSELL OF PIECED BRAIN
QUILTED BY SEW SHABBY QUILTING

Paint Chips

This quilt can easily be made in a day. Just select the fabrics, do a little cutting, and it's off to the sewing machine.

SPECIFICATIONS
Skill Level: Beginner
Quilt Size: 41¾" x 54½"
Block Size: 8¾" x 8¾" finished
Number of Blocks: 6

MATERIALS

- ½ yard each 6 coordinating prints*
- ⅝ yard black print*
- 1⅛ yards white solid
- Backing to size
- Batting to size
- Thread
- Basic sewing tools and supplies

Meow fabric collection by Riley Blake Designs used to make sample.

CUTTING

From 6 coordinating prints:

- Cut 1 (8¼" by fabric width) strip each fabric.
    Trim each strip to make an 8¼" x 30½" A strip.
- Cut 1 (5¼" by fabric width) strip each fabric.
    Subcut each strip into 2 (5¼") D squares.

From black print:

- Cut 6 (2¼" by fabric width) binding strips.

From white solid:

- Cut 2 (5¼" by fabric width) strips.
    Subcut strips into 12 (5¼") C squares.
- Cut 2 (1¼" by fabric width) strips.
    Trim each strip to make 2 (1¼" x 30½") B1 strips.
- Cut 10 (1½" by fabric width) strips.
    Trim 3 strips to make 3 (1½" x 30½") B2 strips. Set aside remaining 7 strips for E/F.

COMPLETING THE BLOCKS

1. Draw a diagonal line from corner to corner on the wrong side of each C square.

2. Referring to Figure 1, place a C square right sides together with a D square and stitch ¼" on each side of the marked line. Cut apart on the marked line to make two C-D units.

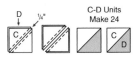

C-D Units
Make 24

Figure 1

3. Repeat step 2 with all C and D squares to make a total of six sets of four matching C-D units.

4. Select four matching C-D units. Join two units to make a row as shown in Figure 2; press. Repeat.

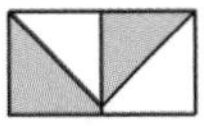

Make 2

Figure 2

5. Join the two rows to complete one Pinwheel block referring to the block drawing; press.

6. Repeat steps 4 and 5 to complete a total of six Pinwheel blocks.

COMPLETING THE QUILT

Refer to the Assembly Diagram for construction steps.

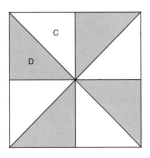

Pinwheel
8¾" x 8¾" Finished Block
Make 6

1. Join the six A strips with two B1 strips and three B2 strips, placing the B2 strips in the middle section, to complete the A-B section; press.

2. Join the six Pinwheel blocks to make a block row; press.

3. Join the E/F strips on the short ends to make one long strip; press. Subcut strip into three 1½" x 53" E strips and two 1½" x 42¼" F strips.

4. Join the A-B section and the block strip with an E strip; press. Add E strips to opposite long sides; press.

5. Sew F strips to the top and bottom of the pieced center to complete the quilt top; press.

6. Create a quilt sandwich referring to Quilting Basics on page 48.

7. Quilt as desired.

8. Bind edges referring to Quilting Basics on page 48 to finish. ●

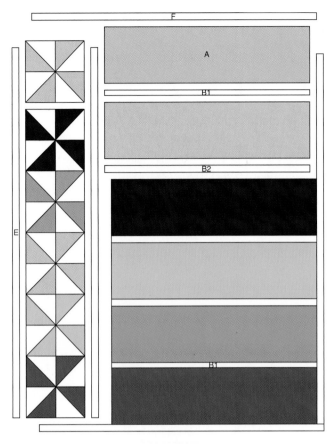

Paint Chips
Assembly Diagram 41³/₄" x 54¹/₂"

DESIGN BY DENISE RUSSELL OF PIECED BRAIN
QUILTED BY SEW SHABBY QUILTING

English Garden

Make this topper this weekend and have it on your table next week. This pattern will complement any decor.

SPECIFICATIONS
Skill Level: Beginner
Topper Size: 50" x 50"
Block Size: 10" x 10" finished
Number of Blocks: 12

MATERIALS

- ⅝ yard dark mustard print*
- ⅔ yard medium peach floral*
- ¾ yard light peach print*
- ¾ yard white solid*
- 1 yard dark mint green print*
- 1⅛ yards dark peach dot*
- Backing to size
- Batting to size
- Thread
- Basic sewing tools and supplies

Sweet Prairie fabric collection from Riley Blake Designs used to make sample.

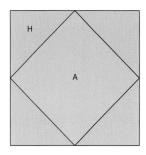

Square-in-a-Square
10" x 10" Finished Block
Make 4

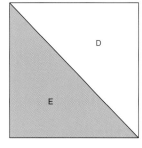

Triangles
10" x 10" Finished Block
Make 8

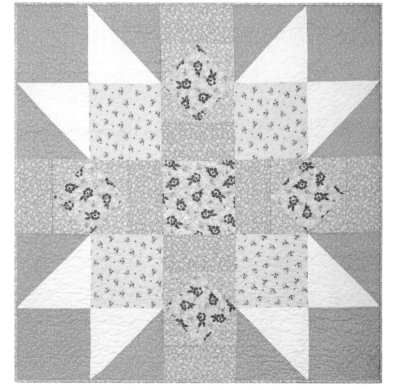

CUTTING

From dark mustard print:
- Cut 3 (5½" by fabric width) strips.
  Subcut strips into 8 (5½" x 10½") C rectangles.

From medium peach floral:
- Cut 1 (7⅝" by fabric width) strip.
  Subcut strip into 4 (7⅝") A squares.
- Cut 1 (10½" by fabric width) strip.
  Subcut strip into 1 (10½") B square.

From light peach print:
- Cut 2 (10½" by fabric width) strips.
  Subcut strips into 4 (10½") G squares.

From white solid:
- Cut 2 (10⅞" by fabric width) strips.
  Subcut strips into 4 (10⅞") D squares.

From dark mint green print:
- Cut 2 (5⅞" by fabric width) strips.
  Subcut strips into 8 (5⅞") squares.
  Cut each square in half on 1 diagonal to make 16 H triangles.
- Cut 6 (2¼" by fabric width) binding strips.

From dark peach dot:
- Cut 1 (10½" by fabric width) strip.
  Subcut strip into 3 (10½") F squares.
- Cut 2 (10⅞" by fabric width) strips.
  Subcut strips into 4 (10⅞") E squares and 1 (10½") F square (4 total).

COMPLETING THE SQUARE-IN-A-SQUARE BLOCKS

1. Sew an H triangle to two opposite sides of A as shown in Figure 1; press.

Figure 1

2. Sew an H triangle to the remaining sides of A to complete one Square-in-a-Square block as shown in Figure 2; press.

Figure 2

3. Repeat steps 1 and 2 to make a total of four Square-in-a-Square blocks.

COMPLETING THE TRIANGLES BLOCKS

1. Draw a diagonal line from corner to corner on the wrong side of each D square.

2. Referring to Figure 3, place a D square right sides together with an E square and stitch ¼" on each side of the marked line; cut apart on the marked line and press open to make two Triangles blocks.

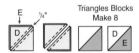

Triangles Blocks
Make 8

Figure 3

3. Repeat step 2 to complete a total of eight Triangles blocks.

COMPLETING THE TOPPER

Refer to the Assembly Diagram for construction steps.

1. Sew a C rectangle to opposite sides of a Square-in-a-Square block to make a C unit; press. Repeat to make a total of four C units.

2. Join one each F and G square with two Triangles blocks to make a corner unit; press. Repeat to make a total of four corner units.

3. Join two C units with the B square to make the center row; press.

4. Join two corner units with a C unit to make the top row; press. Repeat to make the bottom row.

5. Sew the center row between the top and bottom rows to complete the quilt top; press.

6. Create a quilt sandwich referring to Quilting Basics on page 48.

7. Quilt as desired.

8. Bind edges referring to Quilting Basics on page 48 to finish. ●

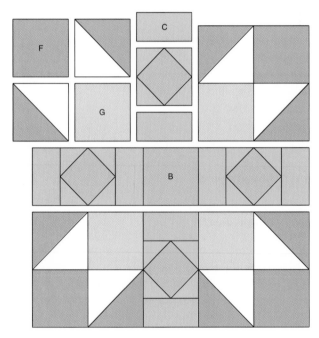

English Garden
Assembly Diagram 50" x 50"

DESIGN BY LYN BROWN
QUILTED BY CATHY O'BRIEN

Gentle Waves

Here's the project for you if you want to finish a quilt in a weekend. All you need is fabric and the desire.

MATERIALS

- 1 yard blue-on-white batik*
- 1 yard light blue batik*
- 1 yard medium blue batik*
- 1⅔ yards dark blue batik*
- 2 yards white solid*
- Backing to size
- Batting to size
- Thread
- Basic sewing tools and supplies

Hoffman California batiks used to make sample.

SPECIFICATIONS
Skill Level: Beginner
Quilt Size: 67½" x 76"

CUTTING

From blue-on-white batik:
- Cut 3 (8½" by fabric width) strips.
  Subcut strips into 23 (4½" x 8½")
  D rectangles.
- Cut 1 (4½" by fabric width) strip.
  Subcut strip into 2 (4½") H squares.

From light blue batik:
- Cut 3 (8½" by fabric width) strips.
  Subcut strips into 23 (4½" x 8½")
  A rectangles.
- Cut 1 (4½" by fabric width) strip.
  Subcut strip into 2 (4½") E squares.

From medium blue batik:
- Cut 3 (8½" by fabric width) strips.
  Subcut strips into 23 (4½" x 8½")
  C rectangles.
- Cut 1 (4½" by fabric width) strip.
  Subcut strip into 2 (4½") G squares.

From dark blue batik:
- Cut 3 (8½" by fabric width) strips.
  Subcut strips into 23 (4½" x 8½")
  B rectangles.
- Cut 1 (4½" by fabric width) strip.
  Subcut strip into 2 (4½") F squares.
- Cut 8 (2¼" by fabric width) binding strips.

From white solid:
- Cut 2 (6½" x 68") K strips along length of fabric.
- Cut 3 (3" x 64½") I strips along length of fabric.
- Cut 2 (6½" x 64½") J strips along length of fabric.

COMPLETING THE QUILT

Refer to the Assembly Diagram for all construction steps.

1. Arrange and join the A, B, C and D rectangles on the short ends with E, F, G and H squares as needed to make 12 same-length vertical rows; press.

2. Join the first three rows to make a three-row strip set; press. Repeat with remaining rows to make a total of four three-row strip sets; press.

3. Join the three-row strip sets with three I strips to complete the pieced center; press.

4. Sew J strips to opposite long sides and K strips to the top and bottom of the pieced center to complete the quilt top.

5. Create a quilt sandwich referring to Quilting Basics on page 48.

6. Quilt as desired.

7. Bind edges referring to Quilting Basics on page 48 to finish. ●

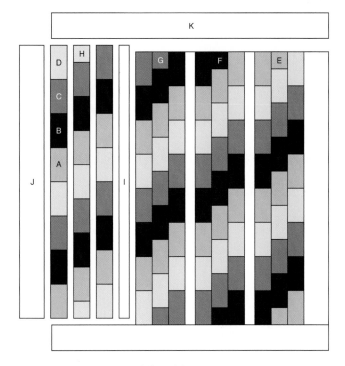

Winter Waves
Assembly Diagram 67½" x 76"

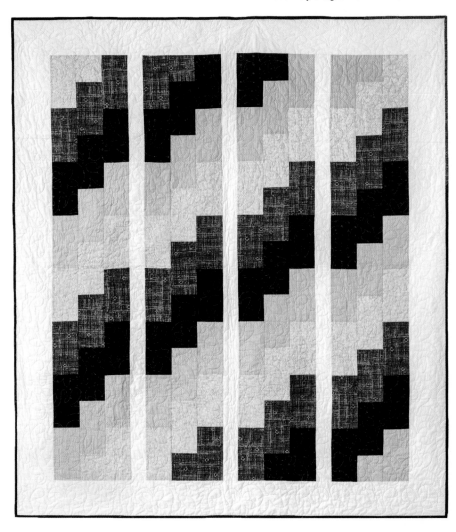

Zoo Review

Arranging half-square triangles in rows in a zigzag formation makes for a stunning quilt that any young person would treasure.

SPECIFICATIONS
Skill Level: Beginner
Quilt Size: 42" x 54"

MATERIALS

- 24 assorted precut 10" squares*
- ⅝ yard green print*
- 1¾ yards white-with-black print*
- Backing to size
- Batting to size
- Thread
- Basic sewing tools and supplies

*Safari Party fabric collection from Riley Blake Designs used to make sample.

CUTTING

From 10" squares:
- Trim each square to make 24 (6⅞")
  A squares.

From green print:
- Cut 6 (2¼" by fabric width)
  binding strips.

From white-with-black print:
- Cut 5 (6⅞" by fabric width) strips.
  Subcut strips into 24 (6⅞")
    B squares.
- Cut 5 (3½" by fabric width) C/D strips.

COMPLETING THE PIECED UNITS

1. Draw a diagonal line from corner to corner on the wrong side of each A square.

2. Referring to Figure 1, place an A square right sides together with a B square and stitch ¼" on each side of the marked line. Cut apart on the marked line to make two A-B units.

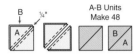

Figure 1

3. Repeat step 2 with all A and B squares to make a total of 48 A-B units.

COMPLETING THE QUILT

Refer to the Assembly Diagram for construction steps.

1. Select and join eight A-B units to make an X vertical row; press. Repeat to make a total of three X vertical rows.

2. Repeat step 1 to make three Y vertical rows, turning units opposite those in the X rows.

3. Join the X and Y rows to complete the pieced center; press.

4. Join the C/D strips on the short ends to make one long strip; press. Subcut strip into two each 3½" x 48½" C strips and 3½" x 42½" D strips.

5. Sew C strips to opposite long sides and D strips to the top and bottom of the pieced center to complete the quilt top; press.

6. Create a quilt sandwich referring to Quilting Basics on page 48.

7. Quilt as desired.

8. Bind edges referring to Quilting Basics on page 48 to finish. ●

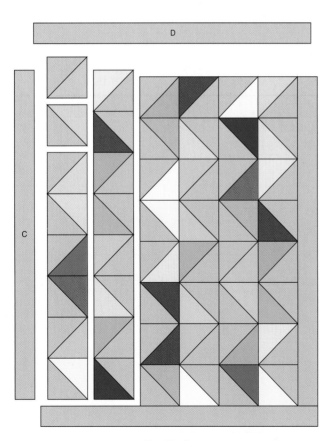

Zoo Review
Assembly Diagram 42" x 54"

DESIGN BY NANCY SCOTT
QUILTED BY MASTERPIECE QUILTING

Leif the Caterpillar Baby Quilt

Got a baby shower coming? Make this lovely quick and easy quilt using a border print.

SPECIFICATIONS
Skill Level: Beginner
Quilt Size: 38" x 48"
Block Size: 5" x 5" finished
Number of Blocks: 20

MATERIALS

- ⅓ yard each coordinating orange, green, yellow, purple and teal prints or tonals*
- ½ yard teal tonal*
- 2¾ yards border print*
- Backing to size
- Batting to size*
- Thread
- Basic sewing tools and supplies

Leif, the Caterpillar fabrics from World of Susybee; Warm 80/20 batting from The Warm Company used to make sample.

CUTTING

From each of the coordinating prints or tonals:

- Cut 1 (6¼" by fabric width) strip. Subcut strip into a total of 20 (6¼") squares. Cut each square on both diagonals to make 80 B triangles.

From teal tonal:

- Cut 5 (2¼" by fabric width) binding strips.

From border print:

- Cut 1 (7") strip along the length of each side of the border print.
   Subcut strips into 2 each 7" x 52" C and 7" x 42" D strips.
   Trim the remaining border print center to make 1 (15½" x 25½") A rectangle.

COMPLETING THE BLOCKS

1. Select four different B triangles to make one Triangles block.

2. Join two of the selected B triangles to make a B unit as shown in Figure 1; press. Repeat.

B Unit
Make 2

Figure 1

3. Join the two B units as shown in Figure 2 to complete one Triangles block; press.

Figure 2

4. Repeat steps 1–3 to complete a total of 20 Triangles blocks.

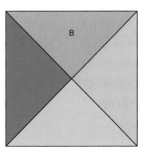

Triangles
5" x 5" Finished Block
Make 20

COMPLETING THE QUILT

Refer to the Placement Diagram for completing the quilt top.

1. Arrange and join five Triangles blocks to make a block strip as shown in Figure 3; press. Repeat to make a total of four block strips.

2. Sew a block strip to opposite sides and the top and bottom of A; press.

Block Strip
Make 4

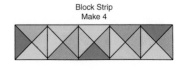

Figure 3

3. Center and sew C strips to opposite sides and D strips to the top and bottom, starting and stopping stitching ¼" from the corners of the pieced center.

4. Referring to Quilting Basics on page 48, miter corners; trim mitered seam to ¼" and press to complete the quilt top.

5. Create a quilt sandwich referring to Quilting Basics on page 48.

6. Quilt as desired.

7. Bind edges referring to Quilting Basics on page 48 to finish. ●

Leif the Caterpillar Baby Quilt
Placement Diagram 38" x 48"

DESIGN BY GINA GEMPESAW
QUILTED BY ANNE COWAN

Picnic Season

Make this quilt today and have it ready for your next picnic.

SPECIFICATIONS
Skill Level: Beginner
Quilt Size: 55" x 73"
Block Size: 9" x 9" finished
Number of Blocks: 35

MATERIALS

- ¾ yard light pink tonal
- 1 yard white tonal
- 1⅛ yards dark green tonal
- 1¼ yards light green print
- 1⅓ yards dark pink tonal
- 1⅝ yards medium pink tonal
- Backing to size
- Batting to size
- Thread
- Basic sewing tools and supplies

CUTTING

From light pink tonal:

- Cut 2 (10¼" by fabric width) strips.
  Subcut strips into 5 (10¼") squares.
  Cut each square on both
  diagonals to make 20 C triangles.
  Set aside 2 triangles for
  another project.

From white tonal:

- Cut 8 (3½" by fabric width) B strips.

From dark green tonal:

- Cut 3 (5⅜" by fabric width) strips.
  Subcut strips into 18 (5⅜") squares.
  Cut each square in half on 1
  diagonal to make 36 D triangles.
- Cut 6 (2" by fabric width) G/H strips.

From light green print:

- Cut 10 (3½" by fabric width) A strips.

From dark pink tonal:

- Cut 2 (10¼" by fabric width) strips.
  Subcut strips into 5 (10¼") squares.
  Cut each square on both diagonals
  to make 20 F triangles. Set aside
  2 triangles for another project.
- Cut 7 (2¼" by fabric width)
  binding strips.

From medium pink tonal:

- Cut 3 (5⅜" by fabric width) strips.
  Subcut strips into 18 (5⅜") squares.
  Cut each square in half on
  1 diagonal to make 36 E triangles.
- Cut 7 (4" by fabric width) I/J strips.

COMPLETING THE NINE-PATCH BLOCKS

1. Sew an A strip between two B strips to make a B-A-B strip set; press. Repeat to make a second B-A-B strip set.

2. Subcut the B-A-B strip sets into 17 (3½" x 9½") B-A-B segments as shown in Figure 1.

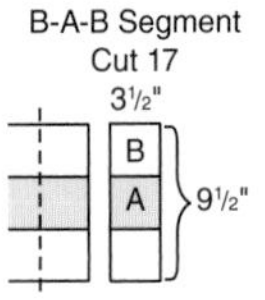

B-A-B Segment
Cut 17
3½"

Figure 1

3. Sew a B strip between two A strips to make an A-B-A strip set; press. Repeat to make a total of four A-B-A strip sets.

4. Subcut the A-B-A strip sets into 34 (3½" x 9½") A-B-A segments as shown in Figure 2.

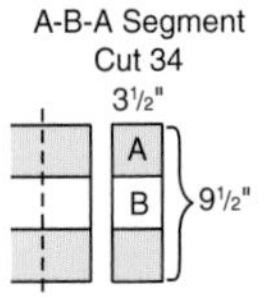

A-B-A Segment
Cut 34
3½"

Figure 2

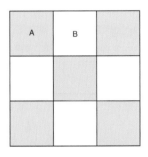

Nine-Patch
9" x 9" Finished Block
Make 17

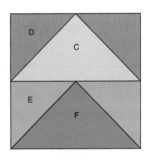

Flying Geese
9" x 9" Finished Block
Make 18

5. To complete one Nine-Patch block, sew a B-A-B segment between two A-B-A segments as shown in Figure 3; press. Repeat to make a total of 17 Nine-Patch blocks.

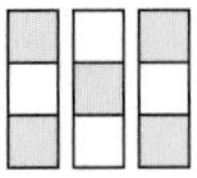

Figure 3

COMPLETING THE FLYING GEESE BLOCKS

1. Sew a D triangle to each short side of C to make a C-D unit as shown in Figure 4; press. Repeat to make a total of 18 C-D units.

C-D Unit
Make 18

Figure 4

2. Sew an E triangle to each short side of F to make an E-F unit as shown in Figure 5; press. Repeat to make a total of 18 E-F units.

E-F Unit
Make 18

Figure 5

3. Join one each C-D and E-F unit as shown in Figure 6 to complete one Flying Geese block; press. Repeat to make a total of 18 Flying Geese blocks.

Figure 6

COMPLETING THE QUILT

Refer to the Assembly Diagram for construction steps. **Note:** *Pay careful attention to the positioning of the Flying Geese blocks in each row.*

1. Join two Nine-Patch blocks with three Flying Geese blocks to make an X row; press. Repeat to make a total of four X rows.

2. Join two Flying Geese blocks with three Nine-Patch blocks to make a Y row; press. Repeat to make a total of three Y rows.

3. Join the X and Y rows to complete the pieced center; press.

4. Join the G/H strips on the short ends to make one long strip; press. Subcut strip into two each 2" x 63½" G strips and 2" x 48½" H strips.

5. Sew G strips to opposite long sides and H strips to the top and bottom of the pieced center; press.

6. Join the I/J strips on the short ends to make one long strip; press. Subcut strip into two each 4" x 66½" I strips and 4" x 55½" J strips.

7. Sew I strips to opposite long sides and J strips to the top and bottom of the pieced center to complete the quilt top; press.

8. Create a quilt sandwich referring to Quilting Basics on page 48.

9. Quilt as desired.

10. Bind edges referring to Quilting Basics on page 48 to finish. ●

Picnic Season
Assembly Diagram 55" x 73"

DESIGN BY NANCY SCOTT
QUILTED BY MASTERPIECE QUILTING

Charming Chains

This bright and fun quilt can be made with precuts. Waste no time cutting and get right to the sewing.

SPECIFICATIONS
Skill Level: Beginner
Quilt Size: 71" x 71"
Block Size: 8½" x 8½" finished
Number of Blocks: 36

MATERIALS

- 36 assorted precut 5" A squares*
- 43 assorted precut 2½" by fabric width strips*
- 2⅓ yards white tonal*
- Backing to size
- Batting to size*
- Thread*
- Basic sewing tools and supplies

Modern Marks fabric collection by Christa Watson for Benartex Contempo Studio; Warm 80/20 batting from The Warm Company; and Aurifil thread used to make sample.

CUTTING

From precut 2½" strips:

- Cut 17 (2½" x 20") binding strips.
- Cut 72 each 2½" x 5" B and 2½" x 7" D strips.
- Cut 36 (2½" x 9") E strips.

From white tonal:

- Cut 6 (2½" by fabric width) strips.
  Subcut strips into 81 (2½")
  C squares.
- Cut 7 (2½" by fabric width) strips.
  Subcut 3 strips into 6 (2½" x 19½")
  F strips; set aside 4 remaining
  strips for G.
- Cut 7 (5½" by fabric width) H/I strips.

COMPLETING THE BLOCKS

1. Sew a B strip to the right edge of an A square to make an A-B unit as shown in Figure 1; press. Repeat to make a total of 36 A-B units.

A-B Unit
Make 36

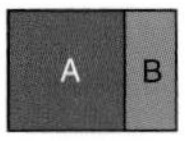

Figure 1

2. Sew a C square to one end of a B strip to make a B-C unit as shown in Figure 2; press. Repeat to make a total of 36 B-C units.

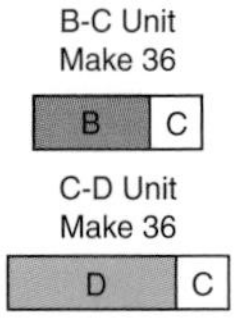

B-C Unit
Make 36

C-D Unit
Make 36

Figure 2

3. Repeat step 2 with C squares and D strips to make 36 C-D units, again referring to Figure 2.

4. Sew a B-C unit to the bottom edge of an A-B unit as shown in Figure 3; press.

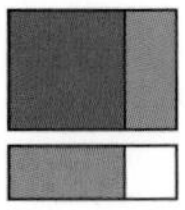

Figure 3

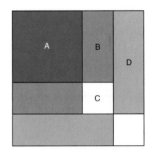

Charm
8¹⁄₂" x 8¹⁄₂" Finished Block
Make 36

5. Sew D to the right edge of the stitched unit and add a C-D unit to the bottom edge to complete one Charm block as shown in Figure 4; press.

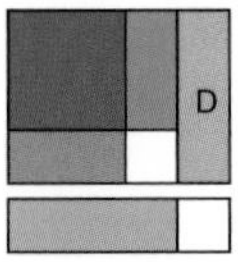

Figure 4

6. Repeat steps 4 and 5 to complete a total of 36 Charm blocks.

JOINING THE BLOCKS

1. Join two Charm blocks with an E strip to make a row as shown in Figure 5; press. Repeat.

Make 2

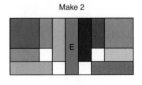

Figure 5

2. Join two E strips with a C square to make a C-E strip as shown in Figure 6; press.

C-E Strip

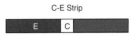

Figure 6

3. Join the two rows with the C-E strip to complete a large block unit as shown in Figure 7; press.

Large Block Unit
Make 9

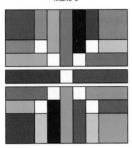

Figure 7

4. Repeat steps 1–3 to complete a total of nine large block units.

COMPLETING THE QUILT
Refer to the Assembly Diagram for completing the quilt top.

1. Arrange and join three large block units with two F strips to make a block row; press. Repeat to make a total of three block rows.

2. Join the G strips on the short ends to make one long strip; press. Subcut strip into two 2½" x 61½" G strips.

3. Join the block rows with the G strips to complete the pieced center; press.

4. Join the H/I strips on the short ends to make one long strip; press. Subcut strip into two each 5½" x 61½" H strips and 5½" x 71½" I strips.

5. Sew the H strips to the top and bottom, and I strips to opposite sides of the pieced center to complete the quilt top; press.

6. Create a quilt sandwich referring to Quilting Basics on page 48.

7. Quilt as desired.

8. Bind edges referring to Quilting Basics on page 48 to finish. ●

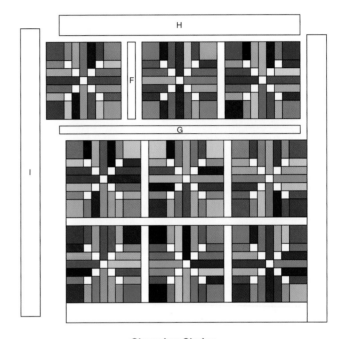

Charming Chains
Assembly Diagram 71" x 71"

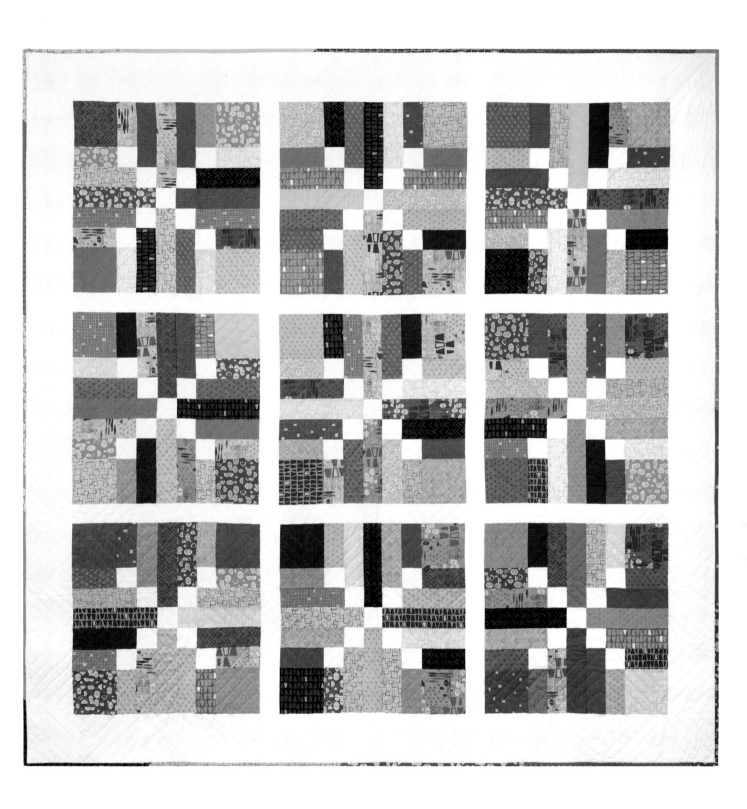

Exploded Block Quilt

Use this quilt for the table, to hang on a wall or as a throw. It has many possibilities.

SPECIFICATIONS
Skill Level: Beginner
Quilt Size: 64" x 64"
Block Sizes: 32" x 16" finished,
32" x 32" finished and
16" x 16" finished
Number of Blocks: 4, 1 and 4

MATERIALS

- 1¼ yards medium brown stripe*
- 1¾ yards dark brown print*
- 2⅔ yards dark cream tonal*
- Backing to size
- Batting to size*
- Thread
- Basic sewing tools and supplies

Autumn Reflections fabric collection for Moda; and Warm & Natural batting from The Warm Company used to make sample.

CUTTING

From medium brown stripe:
- Cut 9 (2½" by fabric width) strips.
  Subcut strips into 2 (2½" x 24½") D strips, 4 (2½" x 14½") M strips and 6 (2½" x 28½") E strips.
- Cut 4 (2½" by fabric width) strips.
  Subcut strips into 12 (2½" x 12½") L strips.

From dark brown print:
- Cut 1 (20½" by fabric width) strip.
  Subcut strip into 1 (20½") A square.
  Cut remainder of strip into 8 (2¼" by remaining fabric width) binding strips.
- Cut 2 (10⅞" by fabric width) strips.
  Subcut strips into 6 (10⅞") H squares.
- Cut 4 (2¼" by fabric width) binding strips.

From dark cream tonal:
- Cut 2 (10⅞" by fabric width) strips.
  Subcut strips into 6 (10⅞") I squares.
- Cut 6 (2½" by fabric width) strips.
  Subcut strips into 6 (2½" x 32½") G strips.
- Cut 8 (2½" by fabric width) strips.
  Subcut strips into 12 each 2½" x 14½" N strips and 2½" x 10½" J strips.
- Cut 3 (2½" by fabric width) strips.
  Subcut strips into 2 (2½" x 20½") B strips and 4 (2½" x 16½") O strips.
- Cut 6 (2½" by fabric width) strips.
  Subcut strips into 6 (2½" x 24½") C strips and 4 (2½" x 12½") K strips.
- Cut 2 (2½" by fabric width) strips.
  Subcut strips into 2 (2½" x 28½") F strips.

COMPLETING THE CENTER BLOCK

1. Sew B strips to opposite sides and C strips to the top and bottom of A as shown in Figure 1; press.

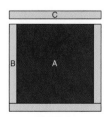

Figure 1

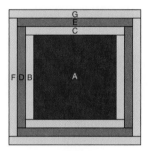

Center
32" x 32" Finished Block
Make 1

Side
32" x 16" Finished Block
Make 4

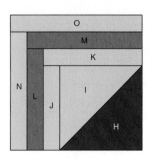

Corner
16" x 16" Finished Block
Make 4

2. Referring to the block drawing, repeat step 1 with D and E and then F and G to complete the Center block.

COMPLETING THE SIDE BLOCKS

1. Draw a diagonal line from corner to corner on the wrong side of each I square.

2. Referring to Figure 2, place an H square right sides together with an I square and stitch ¼" on each side of the marked line. Cut apart on the marked line and press open to complete two H-I units. Repeat with the remaining H and I squares to make a total of 12 H-I units. Set aside four H-I units for the Corner blocks.

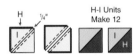

Figure 2

3. To complete one Side block, join two H-I units as shown in Figure 3; press.

Figure 3

4. Sew a J strip to each I end and add a C strip to the light long edge as shown in Figure 4; press.

Figure 4

5. Referring to the block drawing, sew L to the J ends and E to the C side; press. Repeat with N on the L ends and G on the E side to complete one Side block; press.

6. Repeat steps 3–5 to complete a total of four Side blocks.

COMPLETING THE CORNER BLOCKS

1. To complete one Corner block, sew a J strip to one I edge and a K strip to the remaining I edge of one H-I unit as shown in Figure 5; press.

Figure 5

2. Referring to the block drawing, add L to the J side and M to the K side, and add N to the L side and O to the M side of the pieced unit to complete one Corner block; press.

3. Repeat steps 1 and 2 to complete a total of four Corner blocks.

COMPLETING THE QUILT

Refer to the Assembly Diagram for completing the quilt top.

1. Sew a Corner block to each short end of a Side block to make the top row; press. Repeat to make the bottom row.

2. Sew a Side block to the F sides of the Center block to make the center row; press.

3. Sew the center row between the top and bottom rows to complete the pieced top; press.

4. Create a quilt sandwich referring to Quilting Basics on page 48.

5. Quilt as desired.

6. Bind edges referring to Quilting Basics on page 48 to finish. ●

Exploded Block Quilt
Assembly Diagram 64" x 64"

DESIGN BY BEV GETSCHEL
QUILTED BY LYNETTE GELLING

It's a Charm Pack

Put those pretty precut 5" squares to good use with this make-it-in-a-day pattern. All you need besides the precuts, is a coordinating background fabric.

MATERIALS

- 72 precut 5" A squares*
- ⅝ yard black-with-cream print*
- 3⅛ yards cream solid*
- Backing to size
- Batting to size*
- Thread
- Basic sewing tools and supplies

Big Sky fabric collection from Moda; Nature-Fil™ Bamboo batting from Fairfield used to make sample.

CUTTING

From black-with-cream print:
- Cut 7 (2¼" by fabric width) binding strips.

From cream solid:
- Cut 12 (3" by fabric width) strips. Subcut strips into 144 (3") B squares.
- Cut 6 (5" by fabric width) strips. Subcut strips into 4 each 5" x 18½" C strips and 5" x 36½" D strips.
- Cut 6 (5" by fabric width) E strips.

COMPLETING THE PIECED UNITS

1. Draw a diagonal line from corner to corner on the wrong side of each B square.

2. Referring to Figure 1, place a B square right sides together on one corner of an A square. Stitch on the

marked line, trim seam to ¼" beyond the stitched line and press B to the right side.

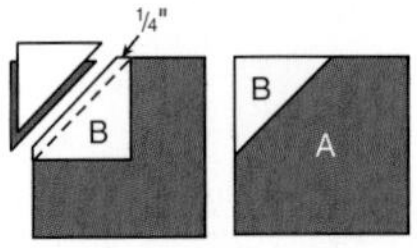

Figure 1

3. Repeat step 2 on the opposite corner of A to complete one A-B unit as shown in Figure 2.

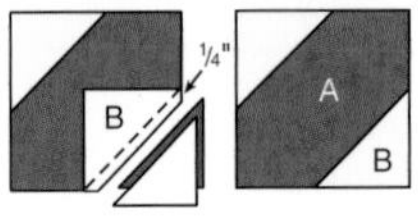

Figure 2

4. Repeat steps 2 and 3 to complete a total of 72 A-B units.

COMPLETING THE QUILT

Refer to the Assembly Diagram as needed for construction steps.

1. Join two A-B units to make an A-B row as shown in Figure 3; press. Repeat to make a total of four A-B rows.

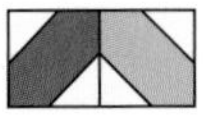

A-B Row
Make 4

Figure 3

2. Join the four A-B rows as shown in Figure 4 to complete the center unit; press.

Center Unit

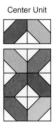

Figure 4

3. Sew C strips to opposite long sides and then to the top and bottom of the center unit; press.

4. Join six A-B units to make an A-B strip as shown in Figure 5; press. Repeat to make a total of four A-B strips.

A-B Strip
Make 4

Figure 5

5. Sew an A-B strip to opposite sides and then to the top and bottom of the center unit; press.

6. Sew D strips to opposite long sides and then to the top and bottom of the center unit; press.

7. Join 10 A-B units to make a long A-B strip referring to the Placement Diagram; press. Repeat to make a total of four long A-B strips.

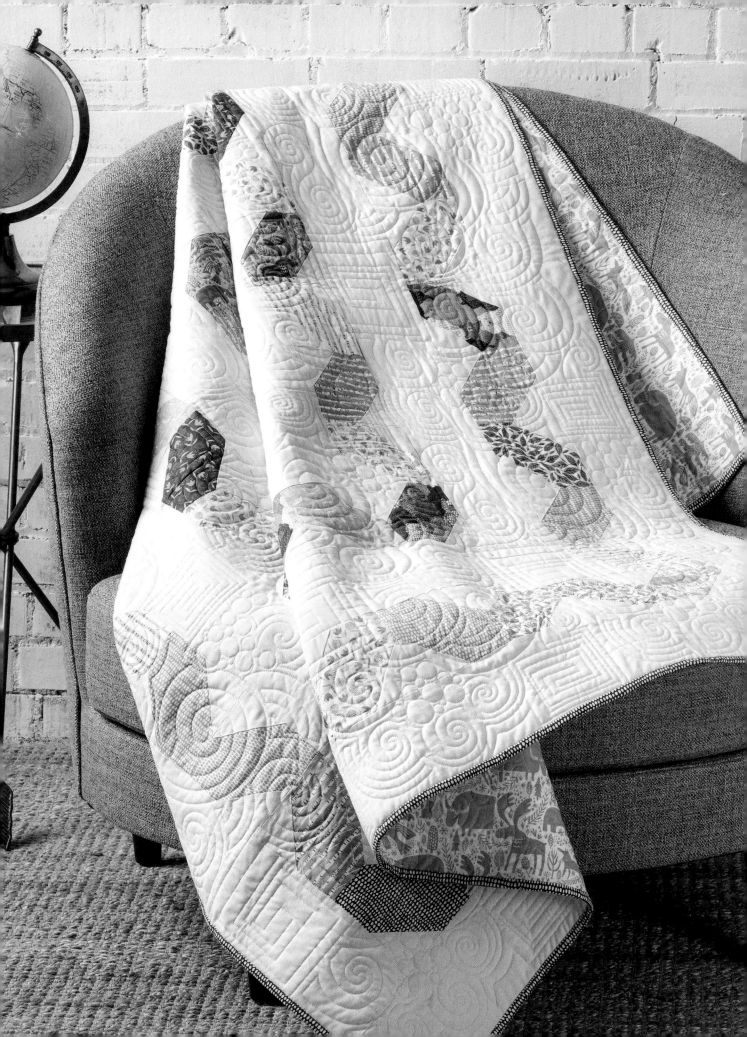

8. Sew a long A-B strip to opposite sides and then to the top and bottom of the center unit; press.

9. Join the E strips on the short ends to make one long strip; press. Subcut strip into four 5" x 54½" E strips.

10. Sew E strips to opposite long sides and then to the top and bottom of the center unit to complete the quilt top; press.

11. Create a quilt sandwich referring to Quilting Basics on page 48.

12. Quilt as desired.

13. Bind edges referring to Quilting Basics on page 48 to finish. ●

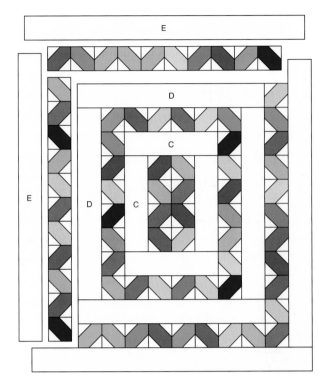

It's a Charm Pack
Assembly Diagram 54" x 63"

Cut-Jewels Runner

Put your favorite charm pieces together with a solid background to create a striking table runner for your next dinner gathering.

SPECIFICATIONS
Skill Level: Confident Beginner
Finished Size: 55" x 16¾"
Block Size: 9" x 9"
Number of Blocks: 4

MATERIALS

- 16 assorted 5" precut squares for A
- ⅜ yard wine tonal
- 1 yard black solid
- Backing to size
- Batting to size
- Thread
- Basic sewing tools and supplies

Here's a Tip

Precut squares are a great way to try out a fabric collection outside your comfort zone without a huge investment.

PROJECT NOTES

Read all instructions before beginning this project.

Stitch right sides together using a ¼" seam allowance unless otherwise specified.

Materials and cutting lists assume 40" of usable fabric width for yardage.

CUTTING

From wine tonal:

- Cut 4 (2¼" by fabric width) binding strips.

From black solid:

- Cut 1 (14" by fabric width) strip. Subcut strip into 2 (14") C squares and 16 (3") B squares. Cut each C square on both diagonals to make 8 C triangles; discard 2.

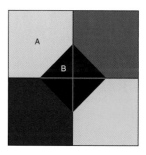

Cut Jewel
9" x 9" Finished Block
Make 4

- Cut 1 (7¼" by fabric width) strip. Subcut strip into 2 (7¼") squares. Cut each square in half on 1 diagonal to make 4 D triangles.
- Cut 4 (2½" by fabric width) E/F strips.

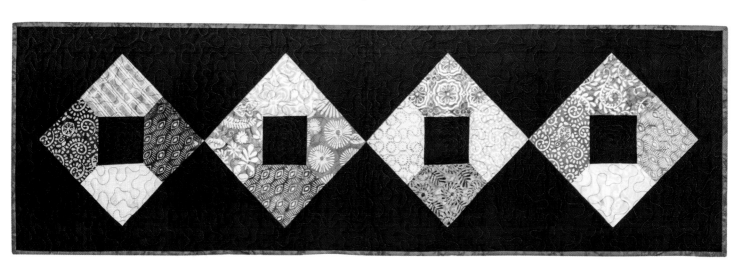

COMPLETING THE BLOCKS

1. Draw a diagonal line from corner to corner on the wrong side of all B squares.

2. With right sides together, layer a B square on one corner of an A square and stitch on drawn line (Figure 1a). Cut ¼" from drawn line to remove excess fabric (Figure 1b). Press B away from A (Figure 1c) to make an A-B unit. Repeat to make a total of 16 A-B units.

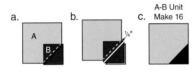

Figure 1

3. Referring to Figure 2, sew four A-B units together to make two rows; press. Sew rows together to complete one Cut Jewel block. Repeat to make a total of four blocks.

Figure 2

COMPLETING THE RUNNER

Refer to the Assembly Diagram for positioning of blocks, triangles and borders.

1. Arrange and stitch blocks with C and D triangles into four diagonal rows; press.

2. Sew pieced rows together to complete the runner center; press.

3. Sew E/F strips together on short ends to make one long strip; press. Cut strip into 2 each 2½" x 51½" E and 2½" x 17¼" F strips.

4. Sew E strips to long sides of runner center and F strips to opposite ends to complete the runner; press.

5. Layer, quilt and bind referring to Quilting Basics on page 48. ●

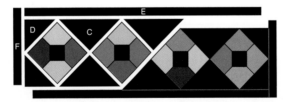

Cut-Jewels Runner
Assembly Diagram 55" x 16¾"

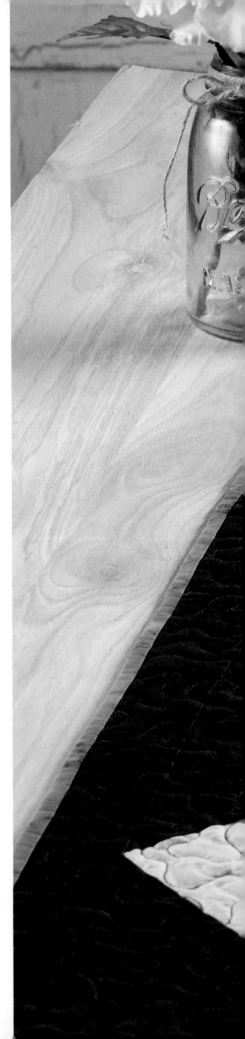

Quilting Basics

The following is a reference guide. For more information, consult a comprehensive quilting book.

Quilt Backing & Batting

We suggest that you cut your backing and batting 8" larger than the finished quilt-top size. If preparing the backing from standard-width fabrics, remove the selvages and sew two or three lengths together; press seams open. If using 108"-wide fabric, trim to size on the straight grain of the fabric.

Prepare batting the same size as your backing. You can purchase prepackaged sizes or battings by the yard and trim to size.

Quilting

1. Press quilt top on both sides and trim all loose threads.

2. Make a quilt sandwich by layering the backing right side down, batting and quilt top centered right side up on flat surface and smooth out. Pin or baste layers together to hold.

3. Mark quilting design on quilt top and quilt as desired by hand or machine. **Note:** *If you are sending your quilt to a professional quilter, contact them for specifics about preparing your quilt for quilting.*

4. When quilting is complete, remove pins or basting. Trim batting and backing edges even with raw edges of quilt top.

Binding the Quilt

1. Join binding strips on short ends with diagonal seams to make one long strip; trim seams to ¼" and press seams open (Figure A).

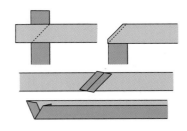

Figure A

2. Fold 1" of one short end to wrong side and press. Fold the binding strip in half with wrong sides together along length, again referring to Figure A; press.

3. Starting about 3" from the folded short end, sew binding to quilt top edges, matching raw edges and using a ¼" seam. Stop stitching ¼" from corner and backstitch (Figure B).

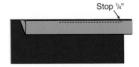

Figure B

4. Fold binding up at a 45-degree angle to seam and then down even with quilt edges, forming a pleat at corner, referring to Figure C.

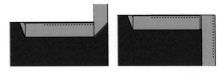

Figure C

5. Resume stitching from corner edge as shown in Figure C, down quilt side, backstitching ¼" from next corner. Repeat, mitering all corners, stitching to within 3" of starting point.

6. Trim binding end long enough to tuck inside starting end and complete stitching (Figure D).

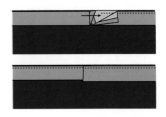

Figure D

7. Fold binding to quilt back and stitch in place by hand or machine to complete your quilt.

Published by Annie's, 306 East Parr Road, Berne, IN 46711. Printed in USA. Copyright © 2019 Annie's. All rights reserved. This publication may not be reproduced in part or in whole without written permission from the publisher.

RETAIL STORES: If you would like to carry this publication or any other Annie's publication, visit AnniesWSL.com.

Every effort has been made to ensure that the instructions in this publication are complete and accurate. We cannot, however, take responsibility for human error, typographical mistakes or variations in individual work. Please visit AnniesCustomerService.com to check for pattern updates.

ISBN: 978-1-64025-105-2
1 2 3 4 5 6 7 8 9